Black and White Rabbit's ABC

Alan Baker

Kingfisher Books

Kingfisher Books, Grisewood & Dempsey Ltd,
Elsley House, 24-30 Great Titchfield Street,
London W1P 7AD

First published in 1994 by Kingfisher Books
2 4 6 8 10 9 7 5 3 1

Copyright © Alan Baker 1994

All rights reserved

BRITISH LIBRARY CATALOGUING
IN PUBLICATION DATA
A catalogue record for this book is available
from the British Library

ISBN 185697 179 1

Cover designed by Caroline Johnson
Phototypeset by Southern Positives and
Negatives (SPAN), Lingfield Surrey
Printed in Singapore

Aa

A is for apple.

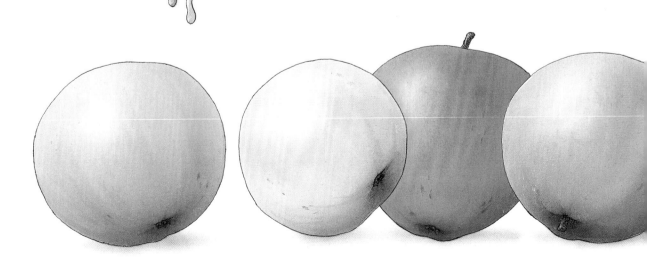

Bb

B is for box,
where Rabbit
puts the apple.

Cc

C is for crayon,
held in Rabbit's paw.

Dd

D is for drawing.

Ee

E is for easel,
to rest Rabbit's
drawing on.

Ff

F is for falling
as the apple
topples over.

Gg

G is for glue,
ooey-gooey
glue.

Hh

H is for hopping,
with a gooey paw.

Ii

I is for ink pot,
right in Rabbit's way.

Jj

J is for jumping,
but not high enough!

Kk

K is for
kicking
it over.
Whoops!

Ll

L is for leaking
all over the floor.

Mm

M is the mess,
soon mopped up.

Nn

N is for nose,
covered in ink.

Oo

O is for
opening
a new pot
of paint.

Pp

P is for the paint,

a bright apple green.

Qq

Q is for
quick!
Paint
in the
drawing.

Rr

R is for
runny,
the
paint's
not
thick
enough.

Ss

S is for
spilling
as paint
drips off
the brush.

Tt

T is for
turning.

Uu

U is for
upside-down.

Vv

V is for very good.
Rabbit's painting
is done.

Ww

W is for water
to wash
the brush.

Xx

X is for kisses
which
Rabbit
draws on his
painting.

Yy

Y is for yawning. What a hard day's work.

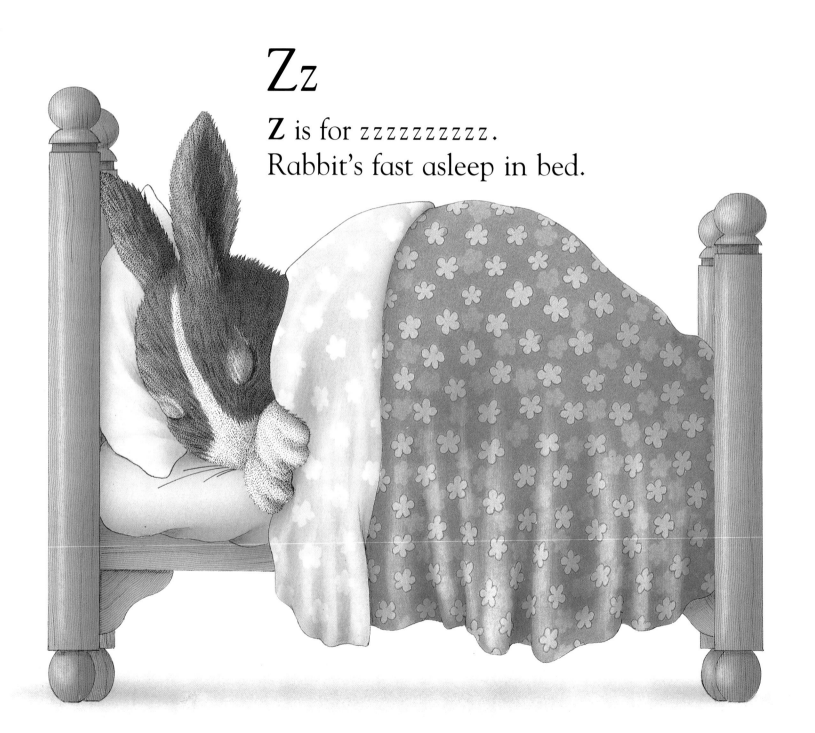

Zz

Z is for zzzzzzzzzz.
Rabbit's fast asleep in bed.